Shine Your Light

Written by
Cindy Della Croce

Illustrated by Simon Mendez

Published by Miriam Laundry Publishing Company
miriamlaundry.com

HC ISBN 978-1-77944-000-6
PB ISBN 978-1-998816-99-6
e-Book ISBN 978-1-998816-98-9

FIRST EDITION

Shine Your Light

is dedicated to grandparents both here and beyond, and to parents, caregivers and educators who lovingly share the invaluable gift of reading with their sweeties!

This book is also dedicated with great love and tremendous gratitude to my fabulous family, forever friends, sensational school family, and the thousands of stellar students who have inspired me to shine my own literary light and finally write the story that's been in my heart for years!

"Grammy!" exclaimed Rosie, as she ran into her Grandma Diana's arms.

Grammy beamed. "My little Rosie! I'm so happy you came to visit."

"Me too!" Rosie said. "I've been counting down sleeps on our calendar."

Grammy, Papa, and Rosie sat sipping sugary tea and munching still warm chocolatey cookies. They talked excitedly about their big plans for the weekend.

5

"Grammy! Grammy!" screamed Rosie in the middle of the night. Grandma Diana had been sound asleep, but now she rushed to Rosie's side. "What's the matter, Rosie?"

"I'm scared those monsters are gonna get me," cried Rosie, pointing to shadows in the corner of the room.

"Oh Rosie," said Grammy. "Those aren't monsters! They are all the stuffed animals you've brought to snuggle with when you come here for sleepovers." Grammy handed Rosie a flashlight from the bedside table.

Rosie shone the flashlight into the corner. Seeing all her beloved toys watching over her, Rosie relaxed.

"See, Honey? When you shine your light, things aren't nearly as scary," Grammy said. "Now, keep this flashlight under your pillow, and try to sleep. We have a big day of fun tomorrow." Grammy kissed Rosie's forehead and tiptoed out of the room.

The next morning, Rosie ate breakfast in the garden. "Look, Grammy!" she called. "I see a bumblebee on that big, pretty flower!"

"That's a sunflower. It's my second favorite flower next to roses," laughed Grammy. "Did you know that when sunflowers are babies, they learn to turn towards the sunlight? Their little faces follow the sun's journey across the sky all day."

"Wow, Grammy. That's so cool!" Rosie exclaimed. "My flashlight is like the sun. So helpful! And with the help of the sun, the flowers are always warm and bright for all the butterflies and bees they attract."

"You're right," agreed Grandma Diana. "And you know what? Your smiling face looks just like a beautiful sunflower."

11

"Papa," sang out Rosie, running into the kitchen. "It's time to go to the beach! Are you done yet?"

"Almost, Miss Rosie. I'm having a bit of trouble with the sink. It's hard to see where the pipe is leaking," Papa explained. "This old fella could use a bit more light down here."

"One sec, Papa!" Rosie raced to get her flashlight and raced back to the kitchen.

She squatted down beside her Papa and shone the light into the dark.

In a few minutes, Papa stood up. "Thank you, my little apprentice," he said. "No more leaks! Your Grammy will finally be happy," he joked, winking at his lovely Diana.

At the beach, Rosie ran in and out of the water and swam with her grandparents.

"Now I want to build a sandcastle," she said. "Like the one over there with the light on top." She pointed across the lake.

"That's a lighthouse," said Grammy. "The light shines day and night."

"But why?" Rosie wondered.

"It guides sailors at night and in bad weather," Papa answered. "When they see that light, they know where they are and avoid dangerous rocks."

Rosie thought about how safe her flashlight made her feel at night, in the dark.

Rosie proudly added the final touches to her sandcastle lighthouse. After a picnic supper, she and Grammy and Papa watched the glorious sunset before leaving the beach.

Back at home with her mom and dad, Rosie found lots of ways to use her flashlight. She shone it...

...into the crisper to find out what cheese was so stinky...

...on her math homework, hoping the solution would appear...

...in Rupert's drooly mouth to examine his fabulous fangs...

...down the cellar steps to see into the spooky darkness.

She shone it...

...under her bed to check for critters...

...in the toilet...

...up her nose.

She even helped her mom write a story!

Then ... the unthinkable, unimaginable, happened...

Rosie's cherished flashlight went

MISSING!!!!

Frantically, Rosie searched everywhere!
She felt lost and scared without her bright,
wonderful, magical light wand.

The next morning, Rosie trudged to the bus stop. She was tired from a very bad sleep. Without her trusty flashlight, there were a lot of scary shadows in her bedroom!

There was one seat left on the bus, beside a boy she had never seen before. His eyes looked even darker and gloomier than Rosie's this terrible morning. Rosie wished she had her flashlight to share with him. They could search for treasure under the bus seat!

Rosie sat down, and taking a deep breath, she mustered up all her happy thoughts of sand lighthouses and homemade cookies. She smiled her brightest smile.

"Hi! I'm Rosie. What's your name?"

"I'm Charlie," he answered shyly.

"Is this your first time taking this bus?" Rosie questioned.

"Yep. My Mom got a new job here, so we just moved in." Charlie's voice quivered a bit. "Today is my first day at your school."

Rosie thought for a moment. She didn't have her flashlight, but maybe she could find another way to shine a light for Charlie. "Want to play before the bell rings? I can introduce you to my friends!"

Charlie sat up a bit straighter and taller, and his eyes didn't look quite as gloomy.

When the bus stopped, Rosie and Charlie jumped off together and ran to the playground.

By the end of the day, Charlie had met lots of new friends.

And Rosie knew that even without her flashlight, there were still lots of ways to shine her light!

Lesson Plan:
Shine Your Light

1. Flashlights and lighthouses are two examples of light sources. Think of other light sources in your home, school, place of worship, and community. Explain how they "illuminate" or light the way for people.

2. Rosie found lots of fun things to shine her flashlight on. If you received a flashlight as a gift, where is the first place you would shine it?

3. Lots of people shine their light! Think of someone that you feel really sparkles and shines their inner light brightly for all to see. Explain HOW they shine their light.

4. Rosie realized that she could shine her inner light and make a real difference in her world! Think of ways you are making a difference in your family, school, neighbourhood and community. How do you shine your light?

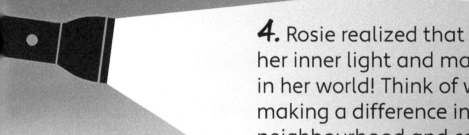

Shine Your Light

(Row, row, row your boat...)

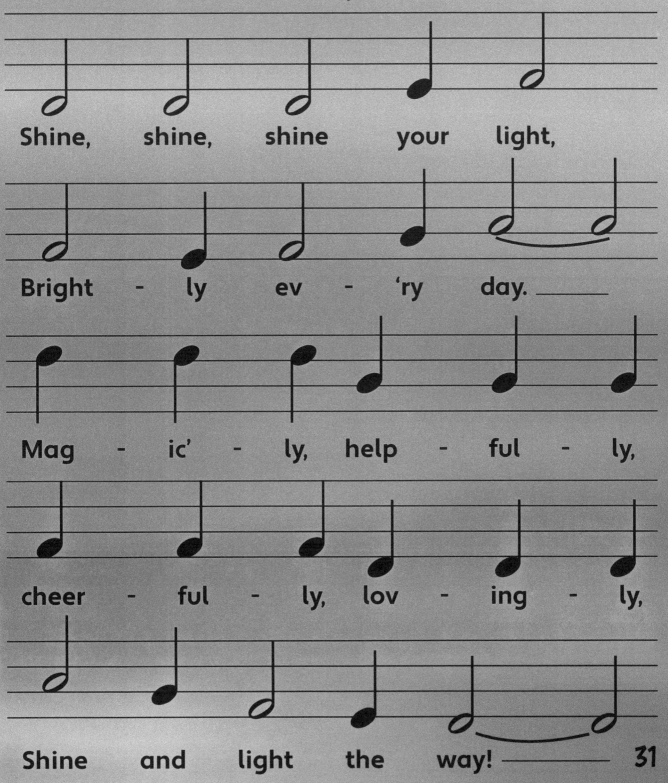

Shine,   shine,   shine   your   light,

Bright - ly   ev - 'ry   day. _____

Mag - ic' - ly,   help - ful - ly,

cheer - ful - ly,   lov - ing - ly,

Shine   and   light   the   way! _____

About the Author

Cindy Della Croce is a first-time author from Guelph, Ontario, Canada. She is the proud mom of three beautiful, inspiring daughters, and is enthusiastically embracing her own brand-new Grammy role!

Cindy's passion for reading and writing shone in her high school English classes and in her elementary library classrooms throughout her 30-year teaching career. Students will remember her motto, "Read, Read, Read," and the Roald Dahl quotation she chose for the library's vibrant sunset mural wall:

**If you have good thoughts
they will shine out of your face like sunbeams
and you will always look lovely.**

About the Illustrator

Simon was born in England with a love of drawing and the natural world. He takes particular pleasure in rendering images in exquisite detail often with an enchanting ethereal quality, conceiving mood lighting and compositions that are dynamic and engaging.

Away from the drawing board, he has a passion for wildlife conservation and spends time exploring the wild world with his wife, kids, and the dog.

Printed in the USA
CPSIA information can be obtained
at www.ICGtesting.com
LVHW060301230923
759035LV00014B/1147